British Library Cataloguing in Publication Data

Base, Graeme
 Creation stories.
 1. Myths. Special subjects : Creation : For children
 I. Title   II. Stewart, Maureen
 291.2′4

 ISBN 0-340-49236-8

Text copyright © Maureen Stewart 1988
Illustrations copyright © Graeme Base 1988

First published 1988 by The Macmillan Company of Australia Pty Ltd, Melbourne
First published in Great Britain 1989

Published by Hodder and Stoughton Children's Books,
a division of Hodder and Stoughton Ltd,
Mill Road, Dunton Green, Sevenoaks, Kent TN13 2YJ

Printed in Hong Kong

CREATION STORIES

Illustrated by
Graeme Base
Retold by
Maureen Stewart

HODDER AND STOUGHTON
LONDON SYDNEY AUCKLAND TORONTO

Contents

How the World was Made

In the beginning there was only water. All the animals were above the water, in a place called Galun'lati. They were happy enough there, but it was very crowded, and they wanted more room.

They wondered what was below the water. At last the little water beetle, Dayuni'si, offered to go and see if it could find out. It darted in every direction over the surface of the water, but could find no firm place to rest. Then it dived to the bottom of the water, and came up with some soft mud, which began to grow and spread on every side until it became the island which we call the earth. It was afterwards fastened to the sky with four cords, but no-one remembers who did this.

At first the earth was flat and very soft and wet. The animals were anxious to get down, and sent out different birds to see if it was yet dry. But the birds came back, because they found no dry place to perch on. At last it seemed to be time, so they sent down the Great Buzzard from Galun'lati, and told him to go and make the earth ready for them.

When he reached the Cherokee country, he was exhausted, and his wings began to sag and strike the ground as he flew. Wherever they struck the ground there became a valley, and where the wings turned up again appeared a mountain. The Cherokee country remains full of mountains even today.

It was still dark when the animals decided that the earth was dry enough to come down, so they got the sun and set it to go in a track every day across the earth from east to west, just overhead.

The Cherokee believe that there is another world under this, and it is like this world in everything — animals, plants and people — except that the seasons are different. The streams that come down from the mountains are the trails by which the Cherokee reach this underworld, and the springs at the heads of the streams are the doorways by which they enter it, but to do this a Cherokee must fast for some days, then go to water, and have one of the underground people for a guide.

When all the animals and plants were first made, they were told to watch and keep awake for seven days and nights, just as young Cherokee people now fast and keep awake when they pray for good health. The plants and animals tried to do this. They were nearly all awake through the first night, but the next night several dropped off to sleep. On the third night others fell asleep, and on the fourth night still more of them fell asleep. This went on until, on the seventh night, only the owl, the panther and one or two more were still awake. To these was given the power to see and go about in the night, so they could prey on the birds and animals which must sleep at night.

People came after animals and plants. At first there was only a brother and sister. Then one day the brother struck his sister with a fish and told her to multiply, and so it was. In seven days a child was born to her, and after another seven days another, and thereafter another every seven days, and there were soon so many there was a danger that the world could not feed them. Then it was made that a woman should have only one child in a year, and it has been so ever since.

The Creation of
the World

The Viking Frost Giants were dark and terrible people, with monstrous shapes and horrible tempers. Two of them were Bor and Old Ymir. Old Ymir's son looked like a glacier and had six heads. He in turn had a son, named Bergelmir. Bor had three sons, Odin, Ve and Vili.

Bor's sons hated the Frost Giant Ymir, and after a battle, they killed him. As they hacked him to pieces, so much blood fell from his body that all his family were drowned except his grandson, Bergelmir, and Bergelmir's wife.

The sons of Bor dragged Ymir's huge body, still pouring and spurting blood, into the middle of Ginnungagap. Ginnungagap was a limitless void of nothingness, a vast abyss of darkness and space. There were so many bloody wounds on Ymir's body that the blood flowing out formed the sea.

Odin, Ve and Vili really destroyed Ymir's body. They slashed, chopped, pushed and pulled his flesh this way and that until they were satisfied with what they had done to his enormous corpse. It was a horrible task.

When they had finished the first part of this gruesome work they had created the ground-work of the earth — rolling plains, hills, dry river beds, empty lakes, and an empty sea bed. They poured Ymir's blood into all the hollows they had created. Now the earth was surrounded by the sea, and had rivers and lakes. Then they hacked and splintered his bones, and from them created mountain ranges. They used his teeth, toes, and the remains of crushed bones to make rocks and seashore pebbles. They used his long, matted hair to make trees, plants, ferns and bushes. They made soil from the rest of his battered flesh.

From the soil a race of dwarfs sprang up. Odin, Ve and Vili, the sons of Bor, realised that although they had created the earth and the sea, they had not yet created the sky. They decided to use the mighty skull of Ymir, now fleshless, and they heaved it up so that it made a dome over the earth. But they had to think of a way to keep it in place.

Now the dwarfs were useful. They ordered four of the stoutest and strongest dwarfs to stand forever at the four corners of the world and hold up the sky. They called them North, South, East and West. Then they threw Ymir's brains into the air, and they became the clouds.

There was a place called Muspellheim, which was a region of fire. Although Odin, Ve and Vili were not often afraid, they knew that the flames from Muspellheim were so tremendous and the heat was so intense that even a million kilometres away it scorched and burnt everything up. Also, to make it even more frightening, the fiercest of the Fire Giants, Surt, stood guard on the flaring hot borders of Muspellheim, gripping a flaming sword of fire in his hand. The hair of Surt was always on fire, shooting out fiery streamers of red-hot sparks in every direction. His head and his face were molten fire and red and orange and purple, and streams of lava, molten hot, poured continuously down his boiling, red-fleshed, misshapen body.

Bor's sons caught the glowing sparks and cinders that came from that fiery place, and put them between the earth and the sky, right in the middle of it all, so that light was given to both heaven and earth.

9

How Pangu Created the World

In the beginning the universe was a dark nothingness, with no night or day. Heaven and earth were as one, and nothing was formed. The universe was a dark, egg-like mass, and in this dark mass the first creature of the universe, Pangu, was born.

Pangu slept in his darkness for thousands of years. As he slept he grew, and when he awoke he was a giant. With a mighty blow he split the dark, egg-like mass apart. The lighter parts of the egg floated upwards and became the sky, and the heavier parts sank downwards and became the earth.

Pangu was worried that the sky and earth might come together again, so he trod heavily on the earth, and reached up and pushed the sky upwards.

When he had finished his mighty task, he was old and weakened, and he slowly died. As he died, his body changed and it changed to create the world we know now. His breath turned into winds and clouds, and his voice turned into thunder. His right eye turned into the moon, and his left eye became the sun.

His body and arms and legs turned into mountain ranges, and his blood became flowing rivers. His long hair and the hairs on his body turned into trees, plants and flowers, and his bones turned into precious stones and minerals. None of his body was wasted — not even the parasites on his skin or his sweat. The parasites became animals and fishes and his sweat turned into dew.

So the great Pangu created the world.

11

Bumba Creates the World

In the beginning, all was dark. There was only darkness and water. Bumba was alone in wet blackness.

Then it happened that Bumba was in terrible pain. This pain would not stop, and Bumba coughed and strained his body, and vomited up the sun. The heat from the sun's rays dried up much of the water, and sandbanks and reefs could be seen, and plains, hills and mountains.

Bumba was still in terrible pain, so he vomited again. This time he vomited up the moon and stars.

Bumba's pain continued. He coughed, strained hard, and vomited up nine living creatures. First he vomited a leopard, named Koy Bumba; then a crested eagle, named Pongo Bumba; then a crocodile, named Ganda Bumba. Then he vomited one little fish named Yo. Then he vomited Kono Bumba, the tortoise, already old in years; then Tsetse, the lightning, which was swift, bright and deadly; then the white heron, Nyanyi Bumba; and one beetle; and the goat, named Budi.

Then Bumba was in pain again, and began to vomit people. The creatures Bumba had vomited up then created other creatures.

Finally Bumba's work of creation was finished. He never felt pain again and had no need to vomit.

Thus we see that from Bumba, the Creator and our First Ancestor, came forth all the wonders of this world.

13

The Birth of the Sun

When the world was very young, many many moons ago, all people had to search for food and water in the dim light of the moon, for there was no sun.

Then came a time when the emu and the brolga were both sitting on their nests of eggs. They argued violently about whose young were better. The brolga, sitting on her nest, became more and more angry, and finally, she could take no more. She left her nest and ran to the nest of her rival, took one of the emu's eggs, and hurled it into the sky, where it shattered against a pile of sticks.

The yolk of the egg burst into a bright yellow flame. The sky people, for the first time, saw the beauty of the world beneath them. They talked together of this beauty, and they decided that the inhabitants below should have more light.

They decided that every night they would collect a pile of dry wood, and set it alight as soon as the morning star appeared. This worked sometimes, but if the day was cloudy, or if there was much rain, no-one could see the star, and no-one lit the fire.

So the sky people thought of another plan. They decided to ask the kookaburra for help. The kookaburra had a strong, loud call, and they asked the bird to call them every morning, so they could light the fire.

So, when the kookaburra's rollicking laughter is first heard, the fire is lit. At first this fire in the sky throws out only a little heat and light. But by noon, the heat can be intense. Later on, the fire begins to die until only a few embers remain to colour the sky.

15

The Creation of Bandicoots and People

In the beginning all was in darkness, and Karora slept under dry ground. Then Karora began thinking and dreaming of things he desired. Wishes and desires flashed through his mind, and, as they did, bandicoots began to come out from his navel and from his armpits. They burst through the soil above and sprang into life.

Soon the sun appeared, and Karora decided to rise and he burst through the earth that had covered him. The gaping hole he left behind became the Ilbalintja Soak. He felt dazed and hungry, so he seized two young bandicoots, and cooked them in the white-hot soil heated by the sun.

His hunger was satisfied, but he needed a mate. So he slept, and while he slept, something emerged from underneath his armpit in the shape of a bullroarer (a carved piece of wood that, when twirled, produces a roaring noise). Soon the bullroarer took on human form, and grew in one night to be a fully-grown young man. This was his first-born son.

Karora sent his son to kill some of the bandicoots, and they cooked them in the sun-glowing soil as before. That night, while Karora slept, two more sons were born to him, again from under his armpits.

The process was repeated for many days and nights. Karora brought to life an increasing number of children and bandicoots from under his armpits.

So it was that the land became full of animals and people.

17

Eurynome and the Universal Egg

In the beginning, there was Eurynome, whose name means 'wide-wandering'. She was the goddess of all things. She came from Chaos, which can be described as an active, barely controllable force. As Eurynome rose up from Chaos, she found nothing solid for her feet to rest upon.

Therefore she divided the sea from the sky, so that there was water and air out of Chaos. She danced, lonely, upon the waves of the sea, and she noticed that her dancing set up a wind behind her. She thought that she would try to create something with this wind, so she wheeled about in her dancing and caught hold of it. She rubbed the wind between her hands, and created the great serpent Ophion.

Then Eurynome took the form of a dove, a sweet, peaceful bird, and brooded upon the water. After some time, she laid the Universal Egg. She directed Ophion to coil his serpent body seven times around this egg, until it hatched, and split in two.

From the egg tumbled out all the things that exist. All the people of the earth tumbled out, of all races and colours. Out tumbled the sun and the moon, so there was light, and the planets and the stars.

The earth tumbled out, with its mountains, plains, hills, rivers and caves. Trees and grasses, plants and flowers tumbled from the egg, and all food-bearing plants.

All living creatures tumbled from the Universal Egg.

19

In the Beginning . . .

In the beginning God created the heaven and the earth. And the earth was without form, and void; and darkness was upon the face of the deep. And God said, 'Let there be light': and there was light. And the evening and the morning were the first day.

And God said, 'Let there be a firmament in the midst of the waters'. And God called the firmament Heaven. And the evening and the morning were the second day.

And God said, 'Let the dry land appear': and it was so. And God said, 'Let the earth bring forth grass, the herb yielding seed, and the fruit tree yielding fruit after his kind': and it was so. And the evening and the morning were the third day.

God made two great lights; the greater light to rule the day, and the lesser light to rule the night: he made the stars also. And the evening and the morning were the fourth day.

And God said, 'Let the waters bring forth abundantly the moving creature that hath life, and fowl that may fly above the earth.' And God created every living creature that moveth. And God blessed them, saying 'Be fruitful, and multiply.' And the evening and the morning were the fifth day.

And God said, 'Let us make man in our image.' So God created male and female. And God blessed them and said unto them, 'Be fruitful, and multiply.' And the evening and the morning were the sixth day.

Thus the heavens and the earth were finished. And on the seventh day God rested.

21

How Earth and Sky were Created

In the beginning there was neither earth nor sky. Shuzanghu and his wife Zumiang-Nui lived above. One day Shuzanghu said to his wife, 'How long must we live without a place to rest our heads?'

Shuzanghu went to his wife, and in due time she gave birth to a baby girl, Subbu-Khai-Thung, or Earth, and a baby boy, Jongsuli-Young — Jongbu — or Sky. But, when the children were born, there was no place for them, so they fell down. They fell to where Phangnalomang the Worm and his wife were living, and the Worm swallowed them both.

Zumiang-Nui tried to find her children, and asked her husband what had happened to them, but he could not tell her. Then she said, 'Next time I have a child, make a clear flat space where I can keep it and set traps all around it.' And so when Phangnalomang the Worm came to devour the next baby, he was caught in one of the traps.

Shuzanghu found him and was so angry that the Worm had tried to eat their new baby that he split his body open. Their first two children were still in the Worm's belly and the one called Sky became the sky and the one called Earth became the earth.

Now Earth and Sky lived together. Sky went to his wife Earth, and she gave birth to a son, Sujang-Gnoi-Rose, and a daughter, Jibbi-Jang-Sangne. These were gods, but they had the shape of mountains. Earth and Sky were pleased that they had created mountains, and after the mountains were born Earth and Sky separated.

23

The Formation of
the Universe

In the beginning, there was only water. In the water swam a monster, a hideous creature with many mouths. The gods Quetzalcoatl and Tezcatlipoca decided that this horrible creature should provide form for the universe.

So the two gods took hold of the monster. They struggled and pulled at its body for days until it was exhausted.

From the lower part of the monster they made the sky and the heavens. From the upper part of its body they made the earth. Mountains and valleys came from its nose, and caves and wells from its eyes. Flowers of all kinds came from its skin, and from its hair came grass, trees, and plants.

Sometimes at night this great earth monster could be heard howling, hungry and angry, crying out for human hearts to eat and human blood to drink. Constant human sacrifices had to be made.

Every year a youth was chosen to be a sacrifice victim. For most of the year he was treated royally, with fine food to eat and priceless clothes. The Aztecs considered him to be a god. Twenty days before the sacrifice he was given four beautiful women as his wives, and for five days before the sacrifice there were festivals.

Then, on the day of the sacrifice, his wives and servants abandoned him. When he reached the stone altar, the priests killed him with a single blow from a stone knife. Then they cut out his heart, still bleeding, and presented it to the sun.

At once a new youth was chosen to take his place, to be honoured as a new-born god, and sacrificed the following year.

24

The Birth of the Plants

Another Aztec story tells of a prince and princess, who were two of the gods, and of their child. They lived in a cave, and were very happy until their child died. The parents buried their child in the ground, the plants grew from his body.

From his hair cotton grew, which provided clothing. From his ears grew all seed-bearing plants, which provided food, and sweet potato grew from his fingers, and maize grew from his finger nails. From his nostrils grew sweet-scented herbs which cured illnesses. All plant life came from the body of the child.

As food and clothing were now available for people, they soon appeared on the earth.

The Birth of the Sun and the Moon

The sun myth tells how the world was once all in darkness. The gods met together and discussed what should be done, and appointed a small god, Nanahuatzin, to give light to the world. Nanahuatzin was not only small for a god, but his skin was covered in scabs and spots. Nanahuatzin accepted his task humbly, but another, boastful god, hoping to win praise and glory for himself, offered to help create life.

The two gods were to sacrifice themselves by walking into a fire. First they were to make offerings to the fire. The boastful god, Teccuciztecatl, offered riches such as precious stones and gold.

Nanahuatzin had little to give — bundles of reeds, thorns stained with his own blood, even scabs from his pimples were his offerings.

When the time came for the ceremony, the great fire was lit.

Teccuciztecatl approached the fire first but, as he felt its scorching flames, he drew back. Four times he walked towards the fire, but every time he retreated from the searing flames. Then Nanahuatzin simply walked up and sacrificed himself to the flames. Teccuciztecatl was so ashamed that he rushed after him and threw himself onto the fire.

Then a great light appeared in the sky. The little pimply god emerged as the sun, and, shortly afterwards, the boastful god appeared as the moon, shining just as brightly as the sun. The gods thought that the boastful god should not shine as brightly as Nanahuatzin so they threw a rabbit up at the moon, to dim its light. Even today, the shape of a rabbit can be seen on the moon.

Rangi and Papa

In the beginning mankind had one pair of primitive ancestors. They sprang from the vast heaven above, and the earth beneath. They were called Rangi and Papa. The world was dark, because they clung together and there was not space for light.

In their warm, dark embrace lay all the human beings they had created, including the gods Tane, Tangaroa, Rongo, Haumia, Tawhiri, and Tu-of-the-angry-face. The children of Rangi and Papa were uncomfortable and restless within their parents' arms, and became so cramped for space they discussed whether they should kill their parents or tear them apart.

Tu-of-the-angry-face wanted to kill them, but Tane argued that they should tear them apart, so that heaven would be above them, and the earth beneath them.

All the children agreed with him except Tawhiri, who was sad at the thought of separating his parents. They argued in the darkness until it was agreed that each son would, in his turn, try to separate the parents. Rongo tried first, and failed, then Tangaroa tried and failed also. All the brothers failed in their turn to separate Rangi and Papa, until finally Tane tried. His arms were too short to use, so he placed his head against his mother, the earth, and raised his feet against his father, the sky, and strained and struggled to separate them. He took no notice of their screaming protests, and he gradually pressed down the earth and thrust up the sky.

Ever since that time Papa and Rangi have dwelt apart, but her loving sighs still rise up to him as mist, and Rangi's tears fall to Papa as dew drops.

How People Were Created from an Egg

In the beginning the universe was water. The waters decided to produce life, so they toiled and boiled with devotion. When they became turbulent and heated, a golden egg was produced. At that time a year, as a period of time, did not exist, but the golden egg floated about for about the space of a year, and so a year was now created and meant a certain period of time.

After the year was finished, a man, Prajapati, was produced from the egg. That is why a woman, a cow, and a mare bring forth their young in the space of a year, because Prajapati was born in a year.

At the end of the year he tried to speak. All children try to speak at the end of one year, because that is when Prajapati did.

All children try to stand at the end of their first year, as Prajapati, the first person, did.